GO!

poetry in motion

poems by
Dee Lillegard

illustrations by
Valeri Gorbachev

Alfred A. Knopf 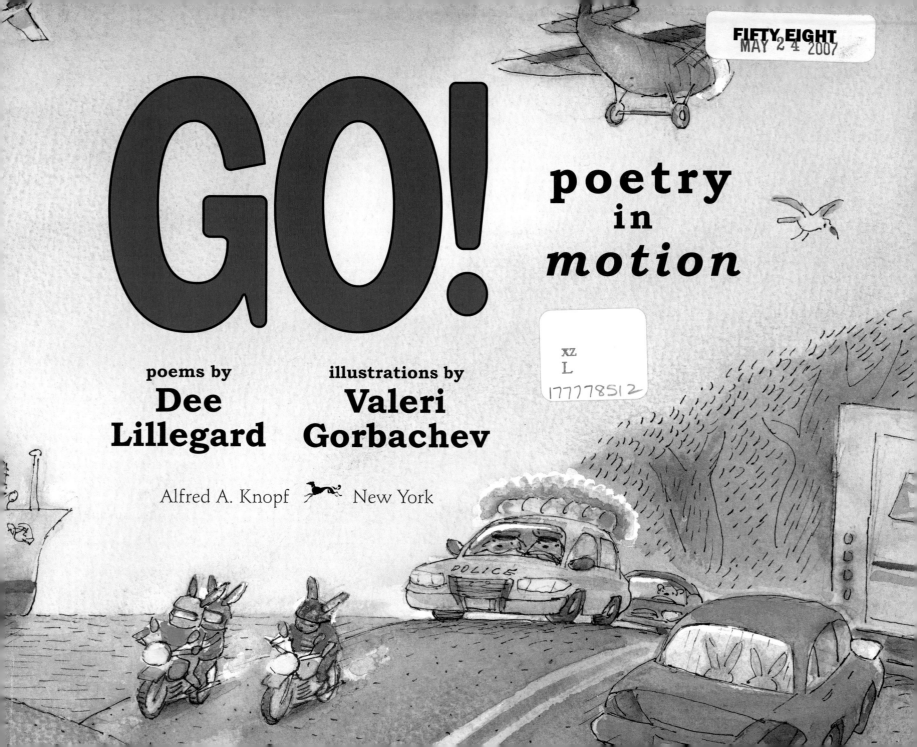 New York

Bike and Trike

Bike teases Trike,
"Bet you wish you were me."
He thinks *two* wheels
are better than *three*!

Scooter

Needs a hand.
Needs a foot.
Or else he'll have to
stay put.

Roller Skates

Lively boots
like how it feels
to *whoosh* around
on little wheels.

Hot Air Balloon
Round, rising,
surprisingly bright,
she floats like a dream
in a feather-light flight. . . .

Skateboard
Just a board on wheels,
but full of *zizz*.
Jump on him
and away he'll *whiz*.

Ice Cream Truck

Chimes a welcome tune . . .
Ice-cold treats
for a hot afternoon!

Lawn Mower

Chewing grass
is all she knows.
She never *moos,*
just mows and mows.

Wheelbarrow
Carries stones, dirt,
wood, a bush . . .
Just needs a push.

Red Wagon
Always getting
dragged behind,
filled and emptied . . .
Doesn't mind.

Roller Coaster

Goes up slow,
but down fast *Oh!*
Like a scary dream,
makes us *scream.*

Ferris Wheel

Rolls around,
but doesn't roll away.
Stays on the ground
while her riders rise and sway.

Merry-Go-Round

Spins lions, zebras,
many a horse,
a jeweled giraffe . . .
and kids, of course!

School Bus
Friendly fellow
dressed in yellow
greets his kids
with a *beep-beep* hello!

Garbage Truck
Our street is clean . . .
he makes it possible
by gobbling trash,
anything tossable.

Mail Truck
Zips down the street
with letters and more.
Delivers . . . delivers . . .
door after door.

Skis

Down snowy slopes
the twin slats slide
in a slippery-dippery
rip-roaring ride.

Ice Skates
Spinning once,
twirling twice—
slipping, sliding *oops!*
on ice.

Sled
Runs down the hill
fast as he can go
till *bump*
he *thumps*
in a pile
of snow.

Pickup Truck

Climbs hills, hauls loads,
bounces over back roads.
You never know where to find him.
But don't worry.
He'll come home,
wagging his tailgate behind him.

Airplane
Up in the air
the metal bird sings,
Look at me.
I've got wings!

Freight Train
Boxcars, flatcars
clickety click click
carry corn, sugar, wheat,
steel, lumber, coal . . .
Click across the country roll
the boxcars, flatcars.
Come see! Come quick!
Clickety click click . . .

Motor Home
Traveling house
likes to stop
to guzzle gas
like soda pop.

Motorcycle
Open and free.
No roof, no door.
Just wind and sun
and a rumbling *roar*.

Moving Van
Takes tables,
couches,
chairs,
beds too,
on the road
to someplace new!

Fire Engine

Fast red truck
quickly arrives
to put out fires
and *save lives*!

Police Car

Lights flash, sirens wail.
Move aside, they say.
Someone's calling.
Someone needs me.
Help is on the way. . . .

Taxi

Knows the city—
her streets, her ways.
Enjoys a passenger
who's polite—and pays.

Helicopter
Propellers whirring
on top of his head,
he can fly forward
or backward instead.

Car
Open the door,
jump in—*slam*.
Off we go
to the traffic jam.

Ship
Dreams of being out at sea,
with schools of fish for company. . . .

Sailboat
Wind-catcher,
water-skipper,
white-sailed
wave-dipper.

Tugboat
Small but tough,
he cheerily chugs
with the ships and barges
he *pushes* and *tugs*.

Speedboat
Sprays and splashes
in daring dashes
across the lake,
leaving waves
in his wake.

Jet
Likes flying at night
over strings of light,
tiny cars all aglow
on the roads below.

For Anthony, Will, Lane,
Natalie, and Granddaddy,
who are always on the go!
—D.L.

To my dutiful partners,
Nancy and Melissa.
—V.G.

THIS IS A BORZOI BOOK PUBLISHED BY ALFRED A. KNOPF

Text copyright © 2006 by Dee Lillegard
Illustrations copyright © 2006 by Valeri Gorbachev

All rights reserved. Published in the United States by Alfred A. Knopf, an imprint of Random House
Children's Books, a division of Random House, Inc., New York, and simultaneously in Canada
by Random House of Canada Limited, Toronto.
KNOPF, BORZOI BOOKS, and the colophon are registered
trademarks of Random House, Inc.
www.randomhouse.com/kids
Educators and librarians, for a variety of teaching tools, visit us at www.randomhouse.com/teachers

Library of Congress Cataloging-in-Publication Data
Lillegard, Dee.
Go! : poems / by Dee Lillegard ; pictures by Valeri Gorbachev.
p.   cm.
ISBN-13: 978-0-375-82387-9 (trade) — ISBN-13: 978-0-375-92387-6 (lib. bdg.)
ISBN-10: 0-375-82387-5 (trade) — ISBN-10: 0-375-92387-X (lib. bdg.)
1. Motion—Juvenile poetry. 2. Transportation—Juvenile poetry.
3. Children's poetry, American. I. Gorbachev, Valeri. II. Title.
PS3562.I4557G6 2006   811'.54—dc22   2005035626

MANUFACTURED IN CHINA • 10 9 8 7 6 5 4 3 2 1 • First Edition